Python for Absolute Beginners

*A Step-by-Step Guide to Mastering Python in **7 Days** with **Hands on Projects***

By

STEM School

This Page Left Intentionally Blank

Contents

Chapter 1

Introduction to Python and Setup

Python is one of the most popular programming languages in the world today, widely recognized for its simplicity, readability, and versatility. It is used in various fields, including web development, data science, artificial intelligence, automation, and, most importantly, physical computing. Unlike low-level languages such as C or assembly, Python provides an easy-to-understand syntax that allows engineers, hobbyists, and students to quickly develop and prototype projects without worrying about complex memory management or syntax intricacies.

Why Python for Engineering and Physical Computing?

Python's role in engineering and physical computing has grown significantly due to its vast ecosystem of libraries and its ability to interact with hardware components easily. Engineers can use Python to control sensors, motors, microcontrollers, and even complex industrial machines. It is widely used in embedded systems, Internet of Things (IoT) projects, and robotics, making it a go-to language for anyone interested in building hardware-based applications.

One of the biggest advantages of Python is its cross-platform compatibility. It can run on Windows, macOS, and Linux, and it is the primary language used in popular single-board computers like the Raspberry Pi. Python simplifies communication with hardware components through libraries like pyserial (for serial communication), RPi.GPIO (for Raspberry Pi GPIO control), and OpenCV (for computer vision applications).

Another significant advantage is Python's vast community and support. Whether you are a beginner or an advanced user, the community offers numerous resources, including forums, documentation, and open-source projects. This strong support system makes learning and troubleshooting easier.

Python is also widely adopted in industries such as aerospace, automotive, biomedical, and telecommunications. Many engineering applications, such as simulation software, automation scripts, and AI-based controllers, rely on Python due to its efficiency and ease of use.

To understand Python's impact, let's look at a comparison of Python with other programming languages used in physical computing:

Feature	Python	C++	Java	Assembly
Ease of Learning	Very easy	Moderate	Difficult	Very difficult
Hardware Control	Easy with libraries	Moderate	Difficult	Direct control

Feature	Python	C++	Java	Assembly
Cross-Platform	Yes	Yes	Yes	No
Performance	Slower than C++ but optimized with libraries	High	Moderate	Very high
Community Support	Extensive	Good	Good	Limited
Use in Engineering Applications	High	High	Moderate	Low

From the table, it is clear that Python offers an excellent balance of ease of use and hardware control, making it a preferred language for both beginners and professionals in engineering and physical computing.

Installing Python and Setting Up the Development Environment

Before diving into programming, it is essential to set up Python on your computer. The installation process is straightforward and depends on the operating system you are using.

Step 1: Downloading and Installing Python

Visit the official Python website at https://www.python.org/downloads/.

Choose the latest stable version of Python. The recommended version is Python 3.x, as Python 2 is no longer maintained.

Download the appropriate installer based on your operating system:

Windows: Download the .exe file and run it.

MacOS: Download the .pkg file and follow the installation steps.

Linux: Most Linux distributions come with Python pre-installed. You can check by running python3 --version in the terminal. If not installed, use sudo apt install python3 (for Ubuntu-based systems).

During installation on Windows, check the box that says "**Add Python to PATH**" before proceeding. This ensures that Python can be accessed from the command line.

Click **Install Now**, and once the installation is complete, verify it by opening a terminal or command prompt and typing:

```
python --version
```

If the installation is successful, it will display the installed Python version.

Setting Up a Development Environment

Python can be programmed using different editors and Integrated Development Environments (IDEs). Choosing the right environment depends on your preference and project requirements. Below are some of the most commonly used IDEs for Python programming.

1. IDLE (Integrated Development and Learning Environment)

IDLE is Python's built-in editor, making it the simplest option for beginners. It comes pre-installed with Python and provides a basic interface for writing and running scripts.

To open IDLE:

- On Windows, search for "IDLE" in the start menu and open it.
- On macOS or Linux, open a terminal and type idle3.

IDLE offers an interactive Python shell where users can test small code snippets. It also includes a basic script editor with syntax highlighting. However, it lacks advanced features such as debugging tools, making it more suitable for simple programs.

2. *Visual Studio Code (VS Code)*

VS Code is a powerful, lightweight code editor developed by Microsoft. It is widely used by Python developers due to its extensive support for extensions and debugging capabilities.

Installing VS Code:

Download VS Code from https://code.visualstudio.com/.

Install the **Python extension** by opening VS Code, going to the Extensions Marketplace (Ctrl + Shift + X), and searching for "Python".

Set up a virtual environment (optional but recommended) using:

```
python -m venv myenv
source myenv/bin/activate  # Mac/Linux
myenv\Scripts\activate  # Windows
```

This helps keep dependencies organized for different projects.

VS Code provides IntelliSense (smart code completion), debugging tools, and integration with Git, making it a preferred choice for larger projects.

3. *Jupyter Notebook*

Jupyter Notebook is an interactive computing environment widely used for data science, machine learning, and prototyping hardware-based applications. It allows users to write code in a cell-based format, making it easy to visualize data and run step-by-step code execution.

Installing Jupyter Notebook:

Open a terminal or command prompt and install Jupyter using:

```
pip install jupyter
```

Launch Jupyter Notebook by running:

```
jupyter notebook
```

This opens a web-based interface where users can create and run Python notebooks.

Jupyter is particularly useful for engineers and researchers who need to document and test their Python code while integrating graphs, images, and real-time results.

Setting up Python and the right development environment is the first step toward mastering Python for physical computing and engineering applications.

Whether using IDLE for simple scripts, VS Code for professional development, or Jupyter Notebook for interactive learning, the choice of environment depends on the user's preference and project complexity.

Writing and Running Your First Python Program

Now that Python is installed and the development environment is set up, it is time to write and execute the first Python program. Python is known for its simplicity, making it an ideal language for beginners and experienced programmers alike. Writing and running a Python program requires understanding how Python scripts work and how they can be executed in different environments such as the command line, interactive shell, and integrated development environments (IDEs) like IDLE and Visual Studio Code.

Creating the First Python Program

A Python program is simply a text file containing Python code. The standard convention is to save Python files with the .py extension. Let's start with a simple program that prints "Hello, World!" on the screen.

The "Hello, World!" program is traditionally the first program beginners write in any programming language. It serves as a basic test to ensure that Python is correctly installed and running. The Python code for this program is:

```
print("Hello, World!")
```

This single line of code instructs Python to display the text "Hello, World!" on the screen. The print() function is a built-in function in Python that outputs data to the console.

Running the Python Program in Different Environments

Python programs can be executed in multiple ways. Each method is suited for different purposes, depending on whether you are running simple one-line commands or complex scripts.

One of the easiest ways to run Python code is through the interactive shell. The Python shell is an environment where users can type and execute Python commands line by line. To access the interactive shell, open a terminal or command prompt and type python (or python3 for some systems). Once inside the shell, type:

```
print("Hello, World!")
```

Pressing Enter will execute the command, and the output "Hello, World!" will be displayed on the screen. The interactive shell is useful for testing small pieces of code and quickly verifying syntax.

For larger programs, Python scripts are written in .py files and executed using the command line or an IDE. To create a script, open a text editor such as Notepad++, Visual Studio Code, or IDLE, type the following code, and save it as hello.py:

```
print("Hello, World!")
```

To run the script, navigate to the directory where the file is saved using the command prompt or terminal and type:

```
python hello.py
```

If everything is set up correctly, the output "Hello, World!" will appear on the screen. Running Python programs this way allows users to write more complex scripts and organize their code efficiently.

IDEs like IDLE and Visual Studio Code provide a more user-friendly way to run Python scripts. In IDLE, simply open the script file and press **F5** or select **Run → Run Module** from the menu. In VS Code, clicking the **Run Python File** button or using the shortcut **Ctrl + Shift + B** executes the script. These tools provide additional debugging and code assistance features, making them ideal for writing and running larger programs.

Understanding Syntax, Indentation and Comments

Python has a clean and readable syntax that is easy to learn and write. Unlike other programming languages such as C, C++, or Java, which use curly braces ₿ to define code blocks, Python relies on indentation. This design choice enforces good coding practices and improves readability.

Python Syntax and Structure

The syntax of a programming language defines the rules for writing valid code. Python has a straightforward syntax that closely resembles natural language. Consider the following example:

```
name = "Alice"
age = 25
print("My name is", name, "and I am", age, "years old.")
```

This program defines two variables, name and age, and then uses the print() function to display the output. Unlike languages such as Java, Python does not require semicolons ; at the end of each statement. The code is more intuitive and easier to read.

Python also allows multiple statements on a single line using a semicolon, but this is generally discouraged for readability. For example:

```
x = 10; y = 20; print(x + y)
```

Although valid, writing each statement on a new line is a better practice.

Importance of Indentation in Python

Indentation refers to the spaces or tabs at the beginning of a line of code. Unlike many other languages, where indentation is optional and only affects readability, Python uses indentation to define blocks of code. This means that proper indentation is required for Python programs to run correctly.

Consider the following example of a conditional statement:

```
x = 10
if x > 5:
    print("x is greater than 5")
    print("This line is also part of the if statement")
print("This line is outside the if statement")
```

In this example, the two print statements inside the if condition are indented, meaning they belong to the block executed when x > 5. The third print statement is not indented, so it is outside the if block and runs independently.

If the indentation is incorrect, Python will raise an error. For instance:

```
x = 10
if x > 5:
print("x is greater than 5")  # Incorrect indentation
```

Running this code will result in an IndentationError. Python enforces indentation strictly, ensuring code structure remains consistent.

Python allows different indentation styles, such as using spaces or tabs, but mixing them within the same program leads to errors. The recommended practice is to use **four spaces per indentation level**, which is the convention followed by most Python programmers.

Using Comments in Python

Comments are non-executable lines in a program that provide explanations and improve code readability. Python supports both single-line and multi-line comments.

A **single-line comment** starts with the # symbol and is useful for short descriptions. For example:

```
# This is a single-line comment
```

```
print("Hello, World!")    # This comment explains the print
statement
```

A **multi-line comment** is written using triple quotes (''' or """) and is useful for documenting functions and complex code sections:

```
"""
This is a multi-line comment.
It can span multiple lines and is often used for documentation.
"""
print("Python supports multi-line comments.")
```

Using comments effectively helps in code maintenance and understanding, especially when working on large projects or collaborating with others.

Python also supports **docstrings**, which are special multi-line comments used for documenting functions and classes. For example:

```
def greet(name):
    """
    This function takes a name as input and prints a greeting
    message.
    """
    print("Hello,", name)

greet("Alice")
```

Docstrings are retrievable using Python's built-in help() function, making them valuable for documenting code.

Writing and running Python programs is straightforward, and Python's simple syntax makes it accessible to beginners. Running Python code can be done through the interactive shell, script files, or IDEs, depending on the complexity of the program. Python enforces readability through indentation, and understanding proper syntax is essential for writing error-free code. Comments play a vital role in making code more understandable and maintainable.

Chapter 2

Python Basics – Variables, Data Types and Operators

Python is a powerful programming language known for its simplicity and readability. Before diving into complex programming concepts, it is essential to understand the basics of Python, including variables, data types, and operators. These fundamental concepts serve as the building blocks for writing effective and efficient Python programs.

Understanding Variables and Data Types

In Python, a variable is used to store data. Unlike other programming languages that require explicit declaration of data types, Python allows dynamic typing, meaning a variable's type is automatically determined based on the assigned value. This makes Python more flexible and easier to use.

For example, assigning a value to a variable is as simple as:

```
x = 10
name = "Alice"
price = 19.99
```

Python automatically recognizes x as an integer, name as a string, and price as a floating-point number. To confirm the type of a variable, the built-in type() function can be used:

```
print(type(x))      # Output: <class 'int'>
print(type(name))    # Output: <class 'str'>
```

```
print(type(price))    # Output: <class 'float'>
```

Python provides several built-in data types. Each type is suited for different types of data and operations. Understanding these types is crucial for writing efficient programs.

Numeric Data Types: Integers and Floats

Python supports two primary numeric data types: **integers (int)** and **floating-point numbers (float)**.

An **integer** (int) is a whole number without a decimal point, while a **float** (float) represents real numbers with a fractional component.

```
a = 42       # Integer
b = 3.1415   # Float
```

Python allows performing mathematical operations on numeric data types, such as addition, subtraction, multiplication, and division.

Operation	Expression	Result
Addition	5 + 3	8
Subtraction	10 - 4	6
Multiplication	7 * 6	42

Operation	Expression	Result
Division	8 / 2	4.0
Integer Division	9 // 2	4
Modulus	9 % 2	1
Exponentiation	2 ** 3	8

Python distinguishes between normal division /, which always returns a float, and integer division //, which discards the decimal part.

String Data Type (str)

A string is a sequence of characters enclosed within either single quotes (') or double quotes ("). Strings are widely used to store text data.

```
text1 = "Hello, World!"
text2 = 'Python is fun'
```

Strings support various operations such as concatenation and repetition.

```
greeting = "Hello" + " " + "Alice"  # Concatenation
print(greeting)                # Output: Hello Alice

repeat_text = "Python " * 3       # Repetition
print(repeat_text)               # Output: Python Python Python
```

Python also allows accessing individual characters in a string using indexing:

```
message = "Python"
print(message[0])  # Output: P
print(message[-1]) # Output: n (last character)
```

Strings are **immutable**, meaning their content cannot be changed after creation. However, new strings can be created through modifications.

Lists – Ordered Collections of Elements

A list is a collection of items stored in a particular order. Lists can hold multiple data types and are defined using square brackets [ ].

```
numbers = [1, 2, 3, 4, 5]
mixed_list = [10, "Python", 3.14, True]
```

Lists allow modification, meaning elements can be added, removed, or changed.

```
numbers.append(6)      # Adds 6 to the list
numbers.remove(2)      # Removes 2 from the list
numbers[0] = 100       # Modifies first element
```

Lists also support slicing, which extracts parts of the list:

```
print(numbers[1:4])  # Extracts elements from index 1 to 3
```

Tuples – Immutable Lists

A tuple is similar to a list, but it is **immutable**, meaning its elements cannot be changed after creation. Tuples are defined using parentheses ( ).

```
coordinates = (10.0, 20.0)
colors = ("red", "green", "blue")
```

Since tuples are immutable, they are useful for storing fixed data, such as coordinates or constant values.

Dictionaries – Key-Value Pairs

A dictionary stores data in key-value pairs, making it efficient for fast lookups. Dictionaries are defined using curly braces {}.

```
student = {
    "name": "Alice",
    "age": 20,
    "grade": "A"
}
```

Values can be accessed using their keys:

```
print(student["name"])  # Output: Alice
```

Dictionaries allow adding, updating, and removing key-value pairs.

```
student["age"] = 21   # Updating a value
```

```
student["city"] = "New York"  # Adding a new key-value pair
del student["grade"]  # Removing a key-value pair
```

Operators in Python

Python supports several operators that perform computations or logical operations on variables.

Arithmetic Operators

Arithmetic operators perform mathematical operations on numerical values.

Operator	Description	Example	Result
+	Addition	10 + 5	15
-	Subtraction	10 - 5	5
*	Multiplication	10 * 5	50
/	Division	10 / 2	5.0
//	Floor Division	10 // 3	3
%	Modulus	10 % 3	1
**	Exponentiation	2 ** 3	8

Comparison Operators

Comparison operators compare two values and return a Boolean result (True or False).

Operator	Description	Example	Result
==	Equal to	5 == 5	True
!=	Not equal to	5 != 3	True
>	Greater than	10 > 5	True
<	Less than	10 < 5	False
>=	Greater than or equal to	10 >= 10	True
<=	Less than or equal to	10 <= 5	False

Logical Operators

Logical operators are used to combine multiple conditions.

Operator	Description	Example	Result
and	Returns True if both conditions are True	(5 > 3) and (10 > 5)	True

Operator	Description	Example	Result
or	Returns True if at least one condition is True	(5 > 3) or (10 < 5)	True
not	Negates the condition	not(5 > 3)	False

Understanding variables, data types, and operators is fundamental to writing Python programs. Python's flexible variable assignments and built-in data types make it easy to store and manipulate data. Arithmetic, comparison, and logical operators allow performing calculations and logical decisions. With this knowledge, the next chapter will explore conditional statements and loops, which enable writing dynamic programs that make decisions and execute repetitive tasks efficiently.

Type Conversion and Type Checking

In Python, variables are dynamically typed, meaning a variable's type is determined at runtime based on the value assigned to it. However, there are times when it is necessary to convert a variable from one type to another. This process is known as **type conversion** or **type casting**. Python provides built-in functions to perform type conversion, ensuring that values are compatible with the required operations.

There are two types of type conversion: **implicit type conversion** and **explicit type conversion**.

Implicit Type Conversion

Implicit type conversion, also known as **automatic type conversion**, is when Python automatically converts one data type into another without any explicit instruction. This usually happens when performing arithmetic operations between different numeric types.

For example, when an integer and a floating-point number are used in an arithmetic operation, Python converts the integer into a float to maintain precision:

```
a = 5   # Integer
b = 2.5  # Float
result = a + b  # Python automatically converts 'a' to a float
print(result)  # Output: 7.5
print(type(result))  # Output: <class 'float'>
```

Python follows a hierarchy when converting types automatically:

- Integers (int) are converted to floating-point numbers (float) if needed.
- Floating-point numbers (float) can be converted to complex numbers (complex) without explicit casting.

Explicit Type Conversion

Explicit type conversion, also known as **type casting**, is when the programmer manually converts a variable from one type to another using built-in Python functions. This is useful when dealing with user input or performing operations where a specific data type is required.

The most common type conversion functions in Python are:

Function	Description	Example
int(x)	Converts x to an integer	int(3.7) → 3
float(x)	Converts x to a floating-point number	float(5) → 5.0
str(x)	Converts x to a string	str(10) → '10'
list(x)	Converts x to a list	list((1,2,3)) → [1,2,3]
tuple(x)	Converts x to a tuple	tuple([1,2,3]) → (1,2,3)
dict(x)	Converts x to a dictionary	dict([(1, "one"), (2, "two")]) → {1: "one", 2: "two"}`

For example, converting a floating-point number to an integer removes the decimal part:

```
value = 7.89
converted_value = int(value)  # Explicit type conversion
print(converted_value)  # Output: 7
```

Similarly, when dealing with user input in Python, input values are always read as strings. If numerical operations need to be performed, explicit conversion is required:

```
user_input = input("Enter a number: ")  # User enters "25"
converted_input = int(user_input)  # Convert input to integer
print(converted_input + 10)  # Output: 35
```

If the input cannot be converted to the required type, Python will raise an error:

```
invalid_input = int("hello")  # This will cause a ValueError
```

To prevent such errors, it is always a good practice to check the type of a variable before conversion.

Type Checking

Type checking refers to verifying the data type of a variable. This is particularly useful when writing functions or handling user input to ensure that the data is in the expected format before performing operations.

Python provides the type() function to determine the data type of a variable:

```
x = 100
print(type(x))  # Output: <class 'int'>

y = 3.14
print(type(y))  # Output: <class 'float'>
```

For more advanced type checking, Python provides the isinstance() function, which checks if a variable belongs to a particular type or a tuple of types:

```
num = 42
print(isinstance(num, int))  # Output: True

value = "Hello"
print(isinstance(value, (int, float)))  # Output: False
```

Using isinstance() is a better approach than comparing type() results directly, as it also works with inheritance in object-oriented programming.

Hands-on Exercise: Creating a Basic Calculator

To apply the concepts of variables, data types, operators, and type conversion, let's build a simple calculator that takes two numbers as input, allows the user to choose an operation, and displays the result.

Step 1: Taking User Input

The calculator needs two numbers as input. Since the input() function returns a string, explicit type conversion to float is required:

```
num1 = float(input("Enter the first number: "))
num2 = float(input("Enter the second number: "))
```

Step 2: Displaying Available Operations

The program should present the available mathematical operations:

```
print("Select an operation:")
print("1. Addition (+)")
print("2. Subtraction (-)")
print("3. Multiplication (*)")
print("4. Division (/)")
```

Step 3: Taking the User's Choice and Performing the Calculation

The user will enter a choice corresponding to the mathematical operation. Based on the input, the appropriate calculation will be performed using conditional statements.

```
choice = input("Enter the operation (1/2/3/4): ")

if choice == '1':
    result = num1 + num2
    operation = "+"
```

34

```
elif choice == '2':
    result = num1 - num2
    operation = "-"
elif choice == '3':
    result = num1 * num2
    operation = "*"
elif choice == '4':
    if num2 == 0:  # Prevent division by zero
        print("Error: Division by zero is not allowed.")
        exit()
    result = num1 / num2
    operation = "/"
else:
    print("Invalid choice. Please select a valid option.")
    exit()

# Display the result
print(f"Result: {num1} {operation} {num2} = {result}")
```

Running the Calculator

Let's assume the user inputs the following values:

```
Enter the first number: 10
Enter the second number: 5
Select an operation:
1. Addition (+)
2. Subtraction (-)
3. Multiplication (*)
4. Division (/)
Enter the operation (1/2/3/4): 3
```

The output will be:

Result: 10.0 * 5.0 = 50.0

Key Takeaways

Type Conversion: Python allows both implicit and explicit type conversion to ensure compatibility between different data types.

Type Checking: The type() and isinstance() functions help in verifying the data type of variables.

Practical Application: A basic calculator demonstrates how type conversion and operators are used in real-world programming.

User Input Handling: Explicit conversion of user input is necessary when dealing with numerical values.

With a solid understanding of type conversion and operators, we can now explore more advanced concepts such as control structures, loops, and functions, which will further enhance our ability to build complex Python programs.

Chapter 3

Control Flow – Conditional Statements and Loops

In any programming language, control flow determines the execution path of a program based on given conditions and iterations. Python provides powerful constructs such as conditional statements and loops, allowing programmers to create dynamic and efficient code. Understanding these concepts is crucial for building decision-based applications, automating repetitive tasks, and improving overall program efficiency.

Conditional Statements: if, elif, and else

Understanding Decision-Making in Python

Computers execute instructions sequentially, but real-world applications often require decisions based on conditions. For instance, a smart home system may turn on lights if it detects motion, or a vending machine may dispense a product only if the correct amount is inserted. Python's **if, elif, and else** statements enable such decision-making by allowing a program to execute specific blocks of code depending on the evaluation of a condition.

Syntax of if Statement

The if statement is used to check a condition. If the condition evaluates to True, the code block under the if statement executes; otherwise, it is skipped.

```
temperature = 30  # Temperature in Celsius

if temperature > 25:
    print("It's a hot day!")
```

In this example, since temperature > 25 evaluates to True, the program prints "It's a hot day!". If the temperature were 20, the statement would be skipped.

Using else for an Alternative Outcome

An else statement provides an alternative execution path when the if condition evaluates to False.

```
temperature = 20

if temperature > 25:
    print("It's a hot day!")
else:
    print("The weather is pleasant.")
```

Since temperature > 25 is False, the program executes the else block, printing "The weather is pleasant.".

elif for Multiple Conditions

The elif (short for "else if") statement allows multiple conditions to be checked sequentially. The program evaluates each condition in order, and as soon as it finds a True condition, it executes the corresponding block and ignores the remaining conditions.

```python
temperature = 15

if temperature > 30:
    print("It's very hot outside.")
elif temperature > 20:
    print("It's a warm day.")
elif temperature > 10:
    print("It's a bit chilly.")
else:
    print("It's cold outside.")
```

In this case, since temperature > 10 is True, the output is "It's a bit chilly.". Even though temperature > 20 is also a condition, the program stops checking once it finds the first True condition.

Nested if Statements

Python allows **nested if statements**, where an if statement is placed inside another if or elif block. This is useful when decisions are based on multiple levels of conditions.

```python
age = 25
has_license = True

if age >= 18:
    if has_license:
        print("You are allowed to drive.")
    else:
        print("You need a driving license.")
else:
    print("You are too young to drive.")
```

Here, the program first checks if the person is 18 or older. If True, it further checks whether they have a license before allowing them to drive.

Loops for Iteration

Loops allow programmers to repeat a block of code multiple times, which is useful when dealing with repetitive tasks, such as processing multiple sensor readings, iterating over a list of data points, or continuously monitoring a system. Python provides two main types of loops: **for loops** and **while loops**.

for Loops

A for loop is used to iterate over a sequence, such as a list, tuple, string, or range of numbers. It executes the loop body once for each element in the sequence.

Basic Syntax of a for Loop

```
for i in range(5):
    print("Iteration:", i)
```

The range(5) function generates numbers from 0 to 4 (excluding 5), and the loop executes five times, printing the iteration number each time.

Output:

```
Iteration: 0
```

```
Iteration: 1
Iteration: 2
Iteration: 3
Iteration: 4
```

Iterating Over a List Using for Loop

The for loop is commonly used to iterate over lists and other collections.

```
fruits = ["Apple", "Banana", "Cherry"]

for fruit in fruits:
    print(fruit)
```

Output:

```
Apple
Banana
Cherry
```

Using for Loop with Strings

Since strings are sequences of characters, a for loop can iterate over each character individually.

```
word = "Python"

for letter in word:
    print(letter)
```

Output:

while Loops

A while loop is used when the number of iterations is unknown and depends on a condition. The loop executes repeatedly as long as the condition remains True.

Basic Syntax of while Loop

```
count = 1

while count <= 5:
    print("Count:", count)
    count += 1  # Increment count to avoid infinite loop
```

Output:

```
Count: 1
Count: 2
Count: 3
Count: 4
Count: 5
```

The loop runs while count is less than or equal to 5. The count += 1 statement increments count in each iteration, ensuring the loop eventually stops.

Using while Loop for User Input

A while loop is useful for repeatedly asking the user for input until they provide a valid response.

```
password = ""

while password != "python123":
    password = input("Enter the correct password: ")

print("Access granted!")
```

The program keeps prompting the user until they enter "python123", then displays "Access granted!".

Break and Continue Statements

Python provides break and continue to control loop execution.

- The break statement **terminates the loop immediately.**
- The continue statement **skips the current iteration** and moves to the next.

Example of break

```
for number in range(10):
    if number == 5:
        break  # Loop stops when number reaches 5
    print(number)
```

Output:

```
0
1
2
3
4
```

Example of continue

```python
for number in range(5):
    if number == 2:
        continue  # Skips printing 2
    print(number)
```

Output:

```
0
1
3
4
```

Understanding control flow is essential for writing efficient Python programs. Conditional statements allow for decision-making based on logical conditions, while loops provide a mechanism to execute repetitive tasks efficiently. By mastering **if, elif, else**, **for loops**, and **while loops**, programmers can write more intelligent and automated scripts. These concepts form the foundation for advanced programming techniques such as data processing, artificial intelligence, and automation.

Advanced Loop Control in Python

Loops are fundamental to programming, enabling the repetition of tasks with efficiency and precision. However, there are situations where controlling the flow of loops is necessary to improve logic and performance. Python provides three essential loop control statements: break, continue, and pass. These statements allow programmers to manipulate how loops execute by either terminating them early, skipping iterations, or providing placeholder functionality for future code. Understanding these statements is crucial for optimizing control flow, particularly in hardware interactions, automation, and real-world applications such as microcontroller-based systems.

The break Statement: Exiting a Loop Prematurely

The break statement is used to exit a loop before it naturally completes all iterations. This is particularly useful when a specific condition is met, and there is no need to continue looping.

Consider an example where a program is searching for a specific number in a list. Instead of iterating through the entire list, it can stop as soon as it finds the target value.

```
numbers = [3, 7, 12, 9, 15, 20]
target = 9

for num in numbers:
    if num == target:
        print(f"Number {target} found!")
        break  # Exits the loop as soon as target is found
    print(f"Checking {num}")
```

Output:

```
Checking 3
Checking 7
Number 9 found!
```

The loop stops when num == target, preventing unnecessary iterations. Without break, the loop would continue checking the remaining numbers, leading to inefficient execution.

The continue Statement: Skipping an Iteration

The continue statement allows skipping the current iteration of a loop while proceeding to the next iteration. This is useful when certain conditions require bypassing execution without terminating the loop entirely.

For example, if a program needs to print only even numbers within a range, it can use continue to skip odd numbers:

```
for num in range(1, 10):
    if num % 2 != 0:  # If the number is odd, skip it
        continue
    print(num)
```

Output:

```
2
4
6
8
```

Here, whenever num % 2 != 0 (meaning the number is odd), the continue statement is executed, skipping the print(num) statement and moving to the next iteration.

The pass Statement: A Placeholder for Future Code

The pass statement serves as a syntactic placeholder. It allows the program to execute without error while keeping the structure intact. This is especially useful when defining functions or loops that will be implemented later.

Consider a scenario where a function needs to be defined, but its implementation is yet to be decided:

```
def process_data():
    pass  # Placeholder for future code
```

Similarly, in loops:

```
for i in range(5):
    if i == 2:
        pass  # This iteration is intentionally left empty
    print(f"Processing {i}")
```

Output:

```
Processing 0
Processing 1
Processing 2
Processing 3
Processing 4
```

The pass statement ensures that the loop runs without syntax errors while allowing for future modifications.

Hands-on Project: Automating LED Blinking Logic

Overview of the Project

In microcontroller programming, LED blinking is often the first step in learning embedded systems. It helps understand how software interacts with hardware. This project involves writing **Python pseudo-code** for an automated LED blinking system, which could later be adapted to work with a microcontroller such as an **Arduino, Raspberry Pi, or ESP32**.

In an embedded system, an LED is controlled by a microcontroller's **GPIO (General Purpose Input/Output) pin**. A program turns the LED **ON and OFF** at specific intervals, simulating a blinking effect. This can be used in real-world applications like status indicators, signaling systems, or IoT-based automation.

Understanding the LED Blinking Logic

To blink an LED, we need to:

1. **Define a GPIO pin** connected to the LED.
2. **Turn the LED ON.**
3. **Wait for a specified time (delay).**
4. **Turn the LED OFF.**
5. **Repeat the process continuously.**

Pseudo Code for LED Blinking in Python

The following Python code simulates an LED blinking process using the time.sleep() function to create a delay.

This can be later adapted to work with microcontroller libraries such as **Raspberry Pi's GPIO library** or **Arduino's MicroPython firmware**.

```python
import time  # Import the time module for delays

led_status = False  # LED is initially OFF

while True:  # Infinite loop for continuous blinking
    led_status = not led_status  # Toggle LED state
    if led_status:
        print("LED ON")  # Simulating LED turning ON
    else:
        print("LED OFF")  # Simulating LED turning OFF

    time.sleep(1)  # Wait for 1 second before toggling again
```

How This Code Works:

- The while True loop ensures that the LED keeps blinking indefinitely.
- The led_status variable is toggled between True (ON) and False (OFF) using not led_status.
- time.sleep(1) creates a 1-second delay between LED state changes, simulating the blinking effect.

Adapting the Code for a Microcontroller

If running this on an **Raspberry Pi**, the LED would be connected to a GPIO pin, and the RPi.GPIO library would be used:

```
import RPi.GPIO as GPIO
import time

GPIO.setmode(GPIO.BCM)  # Use Broadcom pin-numbering
LED_PIN = 18  # GPIO pin number

GPIO.setup(LED_PIN, GPIO.OUT) # Set LED pin as an output

while True:
    GPIO.output(LED_PIN, GPIO.HIGH) # Turn LED ON
    time.sleep(1)  # Wait for 1 second
    GPIO.output(LED_PIN, GPIO.LOW) # Turn LED OFF
    time.sleep(1)  # Wait for 1 second
```

In this code:

- GPIO.output(LED_PIN, GPIO.HIGH) turns the LED ON.
- GPIO.output(LED_PIN, GPIO.LOW) turns the LED OFF.
- The time.sleep(1) function creates the blinking delay.

Real-World Applications of LED Blinking

Traffic Signal Indications: LED lights blink at regular intervals to signal traffic movement.

Warning and Alert Systems: Devices use blinking LEDs to indicate errors or system faults.

IoT-Based Automation: LEDs in IoT projects serve as visual indicators for device status.

Security Systems: Motion-detection systems use blinking LEDs for alerts.

Understanding break, continue, and pass statements gives programmers greater control over loops, making code more efficient and readable. These concepts are highly relevant when working with **hardware automation**, particularly in microcontroller-based projects. The LED blinking example demonstrates how Python logic can be translated into real-world applications, making it a foundational concept for **embedded systems, robotics, and IoT projects**.

Chapter 4

Functions and Modules in Python

Programming is not just about writing lines of code but about organizing and structuring code efficiently. One of the most important principles in Python (and programming in general) is the use of **functions** and **modules**. Functions help break down a complex problem into smaller, manageable parts, while modules allow for reusability and better code organization.

By mastering functions and modules, programmers can write **cleaner, reusable, and more efficient code**. These concepts are particularly crucial when working on large projects, **hardware automation**, or **AI-based applications**, where modularity enhances maintainability and debugging.

Understanding Functions in Python

A function is a **block of reusable code** designed to perform a specific task. Instead of repeating code multiple times, we can define a function and call it whenever needed. This not only improves efficiency but also makes debugging and maintaining the program easier.

A function in Python is defined using the def keyword, followed by the function name and parentheses.

Basic Syntax of a Function

```
def function_name(parameters):
    # Code block (function body)
    return value  # Optional return statement
```

Functions can accept input values (parameters) and return results. If no return statement is specified, the function returns None by default.

Example 1: Simple Function Without Parameters

```
def greet():
    print("Hello, welcome to Python programming!")

greet()  # Function call
```

Output:

```
Hello, welcome to Python programming!
```

This function does not take any arguments and simply prints a message when called.

Understanding Function Parameters and Arguments

Functions can accept parameters, making them more flexible and reusable. Parameters are variables passed to the function when calling it.

```
def greet_user(name):
    print(f"Hello, {name}! Welcome to Python.")

greet_user("Alice")
```

Output:

Hello, Alice! Welcome to Python.

Here, "Alice" is an argument passed to the function greet_user, which replaces the parameter name when executed.

Local vs. Global Variables

Variables inside a function are **local**, meaning they exist only within that function and cannot be accessed outside it. On the other hand, **global variables** exist throughout the program and can be accessed anywhere.

Example 2: Local and Global Variables

```
global_var = "I am global"  # Global variable

def test_scope():
    local_var = "I am local"  # Local variable
    print(local_var)
    print(global_var)  # Can access global variables

test_scope()
```

```
# print(local_var)  # This will cause an error because local_var is
not accessible outside the function
```

Output:

```
I am local
I am global
```

A local variable is only accessible within the function where it is defined. Trying to access local_var outside the function will result in an error.

If a function needs to modify a global variable, the global keyword must be used.

```
counter = 0  # Global variable

def increment():
    global counter
    counter += 1  # Modifies the global variable

increment()
print(counter)  # Output: 1
```

Global variables should be used with caution because modifying them inside functions can make debugging harder in complex programs.

Returning Values from a Function

Functions can return values using the return statement, which allows capturing the output and using it elsewhere.

```
def add_numbers(a, b):
    return a + b  # Returns the sum of two numbers

result = add_numbers(5, 3)
print(result)  # Output: 8
```

This is useful for performing calculations and returning results for further processing.

Working with Python Modules

Modules in Python are **files containing Python code** that define functions, classes, and variables. They help in organizing large programs by breaking them into smaller, manageable parts.

Python has **built-in modules** like math, random, and datetime, which provide useful functionality without needing to write custom code. Additionally, custom modules can be created to group related functions together.

Importing Built-in Modules

Python provides many useful built-in modules that can be imported and used directly.

Example 3: Using the `math` Module

```
import math

print(math.sqrt(25))  # Output: 5.0
print(math.pi)  # Output: 3.141592653589793
```

The `math` module provides mathematical functions such as square root, trigonometric functions, and constants like π (pi).

Creating a Custom Module

A **custom module** is simply a Python file (.py) containing functions and variables that can be imported into other programs.

Step 1: Create a File Named `mymodule.py`

```
# mymodule.py
def greet(name):
    return f'Hello, {name}! Welcome to Python."

def square(number):
    return number ** 2
```

Step 2: Import and Use the Module in Another File

import mymodule

print(mymodule.greet("Alice")) # Output: Hello, Alice! Welcome to Python.
print(mymodule.square(4)) # Output: 16

This approach keeps the code organized and reusable across multiple programs.

Hands-on Exercise: Creating a Simple Math Utility Module

To understand the power of modules, let's create a **math utility module** that provides functions for addition, subtraction, multiplication, and division.

Step 1: Create a File Named math_utils.py

```
# math_utils.py

def add(a, b):
    return a + b

def subtract(a, b):
    return a - b

def multiply(a, b):
```

```
    return a * b

def divide(a, b):
    if b == 0:
        return "Error! Division by zero."
    return a / b
```

Step 2: Use This Module in Another Python File

```
import math_utils

print(math_utils.add(10, 5))      # Output: 15
print(math_utils.subtract(10, 5)) # Output: 5
print(math_utils.multiply(10, 5)) # Output: 50
print(math_utils.divide(10, 5))   # Output: 2.0
```

This method allows keeping all mathematical operations in one file while using them in different programs without rewriting the logic.

Functions and modules are essential for **efficient, reusable, and organized programming**. Functions help in **breaking complex tasks into smaller parts**, while modules allow for **better structuring of large programs**. Understanding **scope** (local vs. global variables) is critical when working with functions, as it defines how data is accessed within a program.

Using Built-in Modules in Python

Python comes with a vast collection of built-in modules that provide ready-to-use functionality, eliminating the need to write common operations from scratch. These modules cover a wide range of functionalities, including mathematical operations, working with time, and generating random values. Understanding these modules is essential for performing complex computations, controlling timing in automation, and introducing randomness in applications like simulations or gaming.

Working with the math Module

The math module in Python provides a variety of mathematical functions that are useful in scientific computing, engineering applications, and physical computing projects. Instead of manually implementing operations like square roots, logarithms, trigonometric functions, and factorial calculations, the math module offers optimized functions that can be directly used.

The module needs to be imported before use. Here's an example of some of its functions:

```
import math

print(math.sqrt(16))    # Square root of 16
print(math.factorial(5))  # Factorial of 5 (5! = 5 × 4 × 3 × 2 × 1)
```

```
print(math.sin(math.radians(30)))  # Sine of 30 degrees
print(math.log(100, 10))  # Logarithm base 10 of 100
print(math.pi)          # Value of Pi
print(math.e)           # Value of Euler's number
```

Commonly Used Functions in the math Module

Function	Description	Example Output
math.sqrt(x)	Returns the square root of x	math.sqrt(9) → 3.0
math.factorial(x)	Returns x! (factorial of x)	math.factorial(4) → 24
math.pow(x, y)	Returns x raised to the power y (x^y)	math.pow(2, 3) → 8.0
math.log(x, base)	Returns the logarithm of x with given base	math.log(8, 2) → 3.0
math.sin(x)	Returns the sine of x (in radians)	math.sin(math.radians(30)) → 0.5
math.cos(x)	Returns the cosine of x	math.cos(math.radians(60)) → 0.5
math.pi	Constant value of π (3.141592653589793)	-

Function	Description	Example Output
math.e	Constant value of Euler's number (2.718281828)	-

Working with the *time* Module

The time module is used to work with time-related tasks such as measuring execution time, adding delays in a program, and getting the current system time. This is particularly useful when working with **hardware automation**, where precise timing is needed, such as blinking LEDs or controlling motors.

Here's an example of using time.sleep() to create a delay:

```
import time

print("Start")
time.sleep(3)  # Pauses execution for 3 seconds
print("End after 3 seconds delay")
```

The time module also allows getting the current system time:

```
current_time = time.time()  # Returns the current time in seconds since epoch (January 1, 1970)
print("Current time in seconds since epoch:", current_time)
```

Using *time* for Measuring Execution Time

A common application is to **measure the execution time** of a function:

```
import time

start_time = time.time()  # Start time
for i in range(1000000):
    pass  # Loop that does nothing
end_time = time.time()  # End time

execution_time = end_time - start_time
print(f"Execution time: {execution_time:.5f} seconds")
```

For applications such as **data logging, time-sensitive automation, or scheduled execution**, the *time* module plays a crucial role.

Working with the *random* Module

The *random* module is used for generating **random numbers**, which is useful in **simulations, gaming, cryptography, and testing automation**. Engineers and developers use randomness for simulating sensor data, generating random test cases, or creating unpredictable patterns in applications.

Here's an example of generating random numbers:

```
import random
```

```
print(random.randint(1, 10))    # Generates a random integer
between 1 and 10
print(random.random())    # Generates a random floating-point
number between 0 and 1
print(random.choice(["Red", "Green", "Blue"]))    # Picks a random
element from a list
```

Using *random* for Simulating Sensor Readings

In real-world physical computing projects, sensors provide values that fluctuate unpredictably. We can simulate this behavior using the random module:

```
import random

def get_temperature():
    return round(random.uniform(20.0, 30.0), 2)    # Simulating a
temperature sensor

for _ in range(5):
    print(f"Temperature reading: {get_temperature()} °C")
```

This script generates random **temperature readings** between 20.0 and 30.0 degrees Celsius, simulating data from a real sensor.

Hands-on Project: Creating a Modular Program to Control Electronic Components

Now that we have explored functions and built-in modules, let's apply this knowledge to a **real-world physical computing project**. The goal is to create a modular Python program that **controls an LED (simulated)**, turning it on or off based on user input.

In an actual hardware project, this could be implemented using a **Raspberry Pi or an Arduino with Python**. For this simulation, we will use simple print statements to represent LED actions.

Step 1: Create a Module led_control.py

This module will contain functions to turn an LED **on or off**.

```
# led_control.py

import time

def turn_on():
    print("LED is ON")
    time.sleep(1)  # Simulating a delay

def turn_off():
    print("LED is OFF")
    time.sleep(1)  # Simulating a delay
```

Step 2: Create a Main Program main.py

The main program imports the led_control module and **simulates user input** to control the LED.

```
# main.py
```

```
import led_control
import random
import time

def simulate_led_control():
    for _ in range(5):  # Simulate LED behavior 5 times
        action = random.choice(["on", "off"])
        if action == "on":
            led_control.turn_on()
        else:
            led_control.turn_off()
        time.sleep(2)  # Delay before next action

simulate_led_control()
```

Expected Output

The program randomly turns the LED on or off five times, introducing **realistic delays** between actions.

```
LED is ON
LED is OFF
LED is OFF
LED is ON
LED is OFF
```

In a **real-world implementation**, the LED can be controlled using a **GPIO pin on a Raspberry Pi**, where turning the LED **on or off** would involve sending HIGH or LOW signals.

Expanding the Project with Real Hardware

This code can be extended to **control a physical LED** using the Raspberry Pi's **GPIO pins** with the RPi.GPIO module.

```
import RPi.GPIO as GPIO
import time

LED_PIN = 17  # GPIO pin connected to LED

GPIO.setmode(GPIO.BCM)
GPIO.setup(LED_PIN, GPIO.OUT)

def turn_on():
    GPIO.output(LED_PIN, GPIO.HIGH)
    print("LED is ON")
    time.sleep(1)

def turn_off():
    GPIO.output(LED_PIN, GPIO.LOW)
    print("LED is OFF")
    time.sleep(1)
```

With this setup, the LED will physically turn on and off based on user commands.

By mastering built-in modules such as math, time, and random, programmers can perform **complex calculations, manage time delays, and introduce randomness into their applications**. The hands-on project provided a **real-world application of modular**

programming, where we built a **simulated LED controller** and saw how it can be extended for **real electronic circuits**. These foundational skills are crucial when working with **hardware automation, IoT devices, and robotics**, enabling developers to build interactive, efficient, and scalable physical computing systems.

Chapter 5

File Handling and Data Processing

Working with files is an essential part of programming, particularly when handling **data storage, logging, or configuration management**. In the realm of **physical computing and automation**, data from sensors, logs of system behavior, or configurations often need to be stored, retrieved, or processed efficiently. Python provides powerful tools for working with different file formats, including plain text files, structured data files like **CSV**, and hierarchical data storage formats such as **JSON**.

Understanding File Handling in Python

Computers store persistent data in files, which are categorized as **text files** (human-readable, e.g., .txt, .csv, .json) and **binary files** (machine-readable, e.g., images, .exe, .bin). Python allows reading, writing, and modifying these files using built-in functions. The process of working with files involves **opening**, **reading/writing**, and **closing** the file after the operation.

The open() function in Python is used to interact with files. It takes two main arguments:

- **Filename**: The name of the file to be opened.
- **Mode**: Defines how the file will be accessed (read, write, append, etc.).

Common File Modes in Python

Mode Description

'r'   Read mode (default). Opens a file for reading. Raises an error if the file does not exist.

'w'   Write mode. Opens a file for writing, truncates the file if it already exists.

'a'   Append mode. Opens a file and appends content at the end without truncating existing data.

'r+'   Read and write mode. Allows both reading and writing to the file.

'w+'   Write and read mode. Overwrites the file if it exists or creates a new file.

Reading from and Writing to Text Files

Writing to a File

Before writing data into a file, the file must be opened in **write mode ('w')** or **append mode ('a')**. Writing mode overwrites any existing content, while append mode keeps the existing content intact.

```python
# Writing to a file
file = open("example.txt", "w")
file.write("Hello, this is a test file.\n")
```

```
file.write("Writing multiple lines is easy in Python.\n")
file.close()  # Always close the file after writing
```

Reading from a File

To read the content of a file, it must be opened in **read mode ('r')**. The read() method retrieves the entire file content, while readline() reads a single line.

```
# Reading from a file
file = open("example.txt", "r")
content = file.read()
print(content)
file.close()
```

Alternatively, using readlines() retrieves all lines as a list.

```
file = open("example.txt", "r")
lines = file.readlines()
for line in lines:
    print(line.strip())  # Removing extra newline characters
file.close()
```

Appending Data to an Existing File

Appending mode allows adding content without deleting existing data.

```
file = open("example.txt", "a")
file.write("Appending new data to the file.\n")
file.close()
```

Using **with** **statement** is recommended for file handling because it automatically closes the file after execution.

```
with open("example.txt", "r") as file:
    content = file.read()
    print(content)  # No need to explicitly close the file
```

Working with CSV Files

Understanding CSV Format

Comma-Separated Values (**CSV**) files store **tabular data** in text format, where each row represents a record and each column is separated by commas. CSV files are commonly used in **data analysis, sensor data logging, and exporting/importing data** between applications.

Here's an example of a **CSV file structure**:

```
Name, Age, City
Alice, 25, New York
Bob, 30, Los Angeles
Charlie, 22, Chicago
```

Python provides the **csv** **module** to handle CSV files efficiently.

Writing Data to a CSV File

To write data into a CSV file, the **csv.writer()** method is used.

```
import csv

with open("people.csv", "w", newline="") as file:
    writer = csv.writer(file)
    writer.writerow(["Name", "Age", "City"])  # Writing header
    writer.writerow(["Alice", 25, "New York"])
    writer.writerow(["Bob", 30, "Los Angeles"])
    writer.writerow(["Charlie", 22, "Chicago"])
```

Reading from a CSV File

To read data from a CSV file, the **csv.reader()** method is used.

```
with open("people.csv", "r") as file:
    reader = csv.reader(file)
    for row in reader:
        print(row)  # Each row is printed as a list
```

Using CSV with Sensor Data Logging

CSV files are widely used in **physical computing projects** for **logging sensor data**. The following example simulates logging **temperature sensor data** into a CSV file.

```
import csv
import random
import time
```

```
with open("temperature_log.csv", "w", newline="") as file:
    writer = csv.writer(file)
    writer.writerow(["Timestamp", "Temperature (°C)"])

    for _ in range(5):  # Simulating 5 readings
        temp = round(random.uniform(20, 30), 2)   # Simulating
sensor temperature
        timestamp = time.strftime("%Y-%m-%d %H:%M:%S")
        writer.writerow([timestamp, temp])
        time.sleep(1)  # Simulating time delay between readings
```

This script generates a **timestamped temperature log**, which can be analyzed later for trends.

Working with JSON Files

Understanding JSON Format

JavaScript Object Notation (**JSON**) is a lightweight format used for **storing and exchanging data** between applications. Unlike CSV, JSON supports **nested data structures**, making it suitable for handling **hierarchical or complex data**.

Here's an example of a **JSON file structure**:

```
{
    "name": "Alice",
    "age": 25,
    "city": "New York",
```

```
    "skills": ["Python", "Data Analysis", "Machine Learning"]
}
```

Python provides the **json module** to read and write JSON files.

Writing Data to a JSON File

To store Python data into a JSON file, the **json.dump()** method is used.

```
import json

data = {
    "name": "Alice",
    "age": 25,
    "city": "New York",
    "skills": ["Python", "Data Analysis", "Machine Learning"]
}

with open("data.json", "w") as file:
    json.dump(data, file, indent=4)  # Indentation for readability
```

Reading Data from a JSON File

To retrieve data from a JSON file, the **json.load()** method is used.

```
with open("data.json", "r") as file:
    data = json.load(file)
    print(data)
```

Using JSON for Configuration Files

JSON is widely used for **storing configuration settings** in automation systems. Here's an example of a **configuration file for controlling a device**:

```
{
    "device_name": "Smart Light",
    "status": "ON",
    "brightness": 80,
    "color": "Warm White"
}
```

Reading and using this configuration in Python:

```
with open("config.json", "r") as file:
    config = json.load(file)

if config["status"] == "ON":
    print(f"Turning on {config['device_name']} at brightness {config['brightness']}%")
```

Understanding **file handling and data processing** is critical in **physical computing, data logging, and automation projects**. While **text files** are useful for storing logs, **CSV files** provide structured tabular data, and **JSON** is ideal for hierarchical configurations. By mastering these techniques, programmers can efficiently manage data storage, transfer, and processing in **real-world applications**.

Data Logging for Physical Systems

Data logging is an essential process in **physical computing, automation, and embedded systems**, where real-time data needs to be recorded and analyzed over time. Whether it is a **temperature sensor, motion detector, light sensor, or any other hardware component**, capturing real-time data and storing it in an accessible format is crucial for **monitoring, debugging, performance analysis, and decision-making**. In various domains like **IoT (Internet of Things), robotics, industrial automation, and scientific research**, data logging plays a critical role in **tracking system behavior** and **improving performance** based on recorded data patterns.

Understanding Data Logging in Python

Data logging involves **collecting, formatting, storing, and retrieving sensor readings or system data** over time. The recorded data can be stored in multiple formats, including **plain text files (.txt), CSV (.csv), JSON (.json), or databases (.db)**. The choice of storage format depends on the use case:

- **Text files** are simple and human-readable but not structured for complex data retrieval.

- **CSV files** store tabular data efficiently, making them ideal for handling numerical data and time-series information.
- **JSON files** are useful when storing structured data with **nested elements**, such as **sensor configurations or metadata**.
- **Databases** (e.g., SQLite, MySQL) are best suited for large-scale data storage and retrieval in **real-time applications**.

Real-Time Data Logging: Hands-on Project

To understand how Python can be used for **real-time data logging**, let's simulate a system where sensor readings are collected, stored, and analyzed over time. The project involves:

- **Simulating a sensor** (for real-world applications, replace with an actual sensor like a DHT11 for temperature and humidity).
- **Logging data into a CSV file** for structured storage.
- **Adding timestamps to each reading** for real-time tracking.
- **Visualizing the logged data** for better insights.

Step 1: Setting Up the Environment

First, install the required Python libraries. If working with actual sensors, additional libraries may be required based on the sensor type (e.g., Adafruit_DHT for DHT sensors).

```
pip install pandas matplotlib
```

Step 2: Writing the Data Logging Script

The following Python script simulates **real-time sensor data logging** by generating random temperature values and saving them in a **CSV file**. In actual applications, the script can read from a real sensor connected to a **Raspberry Pi, Arduino, or other microcontroller**.

```python
import csv
import time
import random
from datetime import datetime

# Define the CSV file name
filename = "sensor_log.csv"

# Open the file in append mode to log new readings
with open(filename, "a", newline="") as file:
    writer = csv.writer(file)

    # Write headers only if the file is empty
    if file.tell() == 0:
        writer.writerow(["Timestamp", "Temperature (°C)"])

    # Simulating data collection for 10 readings
    for i in range(10):
        timestamp        =        datetime.now().strftime("%Y-%m-%d
%H:%M:%S")
        temperature  =  round(random.uniform(20,  35),  2)     #
Simulated temperature reading
```

```
# Writing data to CSV file
writer.writerow([timestamp, temperature])
print(f"Logged: {timestamp} - {temperature}°C")

# Wait for 2 seconds before next reading
time.sleep(2)
```

Step 3: Verifying the Logged Data

After running the script, open **sensor_log.csv** and check if data is being logged correctly. The file should have **structured tabular data** like this:

Timestamp	Temperature (°C)
2025-02-24 14:30:01	23.5
2025-02-24 14:30:03	24.1
2025-02-24 14:30:05	25.7
2025-02-24 14:30:07	22.9
2025-02-24 14:30:09	23.8

Step 4: Visualizing the Logged Data

To analyze the data, plotting it using **Matplotlib** can provide useful insights. The following script reads the logged data and plots a **temperature-time graph**.

```
import pandas as pd
import matplotlib.pyplot as plt

# Load the logged data
data = pd.read_csv("sensor_log.csv")

# Convert timestamp to datetime format
data["Timestamp"] = pd.to_datetime(data["Timestamp"])

# Plot the temperature trend
plt.figure(figsize=(10, 5))
plt.plot(data["Timestamp"], data["Temperature (°C)"], marker="o",
linestyle="-", color="b", label="Temperature")
plt.xlabel("Time")
plt.ylabel("Temperature (°C)")
plt.title("Temperature Sensor Readings Over Time")
plt.xticks(rotation=45)
plt.legend()
plt.grid()
plt.show()
```

Using Real Sensors for Data Logging

For real-world applications, replace the **simulated sensor** with an actual sensor like a **DHT11 (temperature & humidity sensor)**. Below is a Python script that logs real-time temperature readings from a **DHT11 sensor connected to a Raspberry Pi**.

```
import Adafruit_DHT
import csv
import time
```

```python
from datetime import datetime

# Set up the sensor
SENSOR = Adafruit_DHT.DHT11
PIN = 4  # GPIO pin where the sensor is connected

# CSV file to store data
filename = "real_sensor_log.csv"

with open(filename, "a", newline="") as file:
    writer = csv.writer(file)

    # Write headers if the file is empty
    if file.tell() == 0:
        writer.writerow(["Timestamp", "Temperature (°C)", "Humidity (%)"])

    for i in range(10):
        timestamp = datetime.now().strftime("%Y-%m-%d %H:%M:%S")
        humidity, temperature = Adafruit_DHT.read_retry(SENSOR, PIN)

        if temperature is not None and humidity is not None:
            writer.writerow([timestamp, round(temperature, 2), round(humidity, 2)])
            print(f"Logged: {timestamp} - Temp: {temperature}°C, Humidity: {humidity}%")
        else:
            print("Failed to retrieve data from sensor")

        time.sleep(2)  # Wait for 2 seconds before the next reading
```

Data logging is a **fundamental concept** in real-world applications, enabling **system monitoring, diagnostics, performance optimization, and automation**. By leveraging Python's built-in **file handling capabilities**, sensor readings can be **stored, processed, and visualized efficiently**.

This chapter introduced **real-time data logging using CSV files**, demonstrated **how to visualize logged data**, and provided **an approach to working with real sensors**. Understanding these techniques allows hobbyists, engineers, and developers to **create data-driven physical computing projects**, whether it is for **home automation, industrial monitoring, weather tracking, or IoT applications**.

Chapter 6

Object-Oriented Programming (OOP) in Python

Python is a versatile programming language that supports multiple paradigms, including **procedural, functional, and object-oriented programming (OOP)**. Among these, **OOP is one of the most powerful and widely used paradigms** because it allows for better code organization, reuse, scalability, and abstraction. In real-world applications, OOP is used extensively in fields like **robotics, embedded systems, game development, IoT applications, and GUI development**.

By using OOP, a programmer can model real-world entities in code, making it easier to manage complex projects involving **hardware components, sensors, and automation systems**. In this chapter, we will explore **OOP fundamentals**, including **classes, objects, methods, encapsulation, inheritance, and polymorphism**, while demonstrating how these concepts can be applied in physical computing projects.

Understanding Classes and Objects in Python

A **class** is a blueprint for creating objects. It defines a **template** containing attributes (**variables**) and behaviors (**methods**) that an object will have. An **object** is an instance of a class, meaning it is an **actual entity created based on the class definition**.

For example, if we are designing an **automated home lighting system**, we might define a class called Light, where each **light** in the system is an object with properties like status (ON/OFF) and methods like turn_on() and turn_off().

Creating a Class and Object in Python

Let's define a simple Python class that represents a basic electronic component **(LED Light)**.

```
class Light:
    def __init__(self, status="OFF"):  # Constructor method
        self.status = status  # Instance variable to hold light status

    def turn_on(self):  # Method to turn the light ON
        self.status = "ON"
        print("Light is now ON")

    def turn_off(self):  # Method to turn the light OFF
        self.status = "OFF"
        print("Light is now OFF")
```

Now, let's create an **object** (instance) of the Light class and use its methods to control the light.

```
# Creating an object of the Light class
led = Light()

# Turning the light ON and OFF using methods
led.turn_on()
led.turn_off()
```

When this code runs, it will output:

Light is now ON
Light is now OFF

Encapsulation: Protecting Data

Encapsulation is a fundamental OOP principle that **restricts direct access to an object's data and ensures that modifications happen through controlled mechanisms**. In Python, encapsulation is achieved using **private variables and getter/setter methods**.

For example, let's modify our Light class to make the status variable **private**, meaning it cannot be accessed directly outside the class.

```
class Light:
    def __init__(self):
        self.__status = "OFF"  # Private variable (cannot be accessed directly)

    def turn_on(self):
        self.__status = "ON"
        print("Light is now ON")

    def turn_off(self):
        self.__status = "OFF"
        print("Light is now OFF")

    def get_status(self):  # Getter method to access private variable
```

```
        return self.__status
```

If we try to access led.__status directly, Python will raise an **AttributeError**. Instead, we must use the get_status() method.

```
led = Light()
led.turn_on()
print("Current Status:", led.get_status())  # Correct way to access
private data
```

Inheritance: Reusing Code

Inheritance allows one class to **inherit properties and methods** from another, enabling **code reuse and hierarchy-based structures**. Suppose we extend our Light class to create a **SmartLight** that includes **brightness control**. Instead of rewriting everything, we can inherit from the Light class.

```
class SmartLight(Light):  # SmartLight inherits from Light
    def __init__(self):
        super().__init__()  # Call parent constructor
        self.brightness = 50  # Default brightness level (0-100)

    def set_brightness(self, level):
        if 0 <= level <= 100:
            self.brightness = level
            print(f"Brightness set to {level}%")
        else:
            print("Invalid brightness level. Must be between 0 and
100.")
```

Now, let's create a SmartLight object and use both **inherited and new methods**.

```
smart_led = SmartLight()
smart_led.turn_on()  # Inherited method from Light class
smart_led.set_brightness(75)  # New method in SmartLight class
```

Output:

```
Light is now ON
Brightness set to 75%
```

Polymorphism: Flexibility in Action

Polymorphism allows different classes to **implement the same method in different ways**, making the code more flexible and extensible. Suppose we have multiple electronic components like **LED, Buzzer, and Motor**, and each of them has a method activate(). Even though the method name is the same, the behavior will be different for each component.

```
class Light:
    def activate(self):
        print("Light turned ON")

class Buzzer:
    def activate(self):
        print("Buzzer is beeping")

class Motor:
    def activate(self):
```

```
    print("Motor started spinning")

# Demonstrating polymorphism
devices = [Light(), Buzzer(), Motor()]

for device in devices:
    device.activate()   # Calls the appropriate method based on object type
```

Output:

```
Light turned ON
Buzzer is beeping
Motor started spinning
```

Hands-on Project: Smart Home Device Controller

Now that we understand OOP concepts, let's create a **smart home device controller** that can manage multiple devices (lights, fans, and buzzers) using Python's OOP features.

Step 1: Defining the Base Device Class

```
class Device:
    def __init__(self, name):
        self.name = name
        self.status = "OFF"

    def turn_on(self):
        self.status = "ON"
        print(f'{self.name} is now ON")

    def turn_off(self):
```

```python
        self.status = "OFF"
        print(f"{self.name} is now OFF")
```

Step 2: Extending the Class for Specific Devices

```python
class Light(Device):
    def __init__(self, name, brightness=50):
        super().__init__(name)
        self.brightness = brightness

    def set_brightness(self, level):
        if 0 <= level <= 100:
            self.brightness = level
            print(f"{self.name} brightness set to {level}%")
        else:
            print("Invalid brightness level.")

class Fan(Device):
    def __init__(self, name, speed=1):
        super().__init__(name)
        self.speed = speed

    def set_speed(self, level):
        if 1 <= level <= 5:
            self.speed = level
            print(f"{self.name} speed set to level {level}")
        else:
            print("Invalid speed level.")
```

Step 3: Creating and Controlling Devices

```python
# Creating smart home devices
```

```
living_room_light = Light("Living Room Light")
bedroom_fan = Fan("Bedroom Fan")

# Controlling the devices
living_room_light.turn_on()
living_room_light.set_brightness(80)

bedroom_fan.turn_on()
bedroom_fan.set_speed(3)
```

Output:

```
Living Room Light is now ON
Living Room Light brightness set to 80%
Bedroom Fan is now ON
Bedroom Fan speed set to level 3
```

Object-Oriented Programming (OOP) is a crucial concept for **organizing, scaling, and reusing code** in Python. In real-world applications, OOP enables the efficient management of **hardware components, automation systems, and embedded applications**.

Using OOP for Structuring Larger Programs

Object-Oriented Programming (OOP) plays a crucial role in structuring larger programs by allowing developers to design complex applications in a modular, reusable, and scalable manner. As software projects grow in size and complexity, traditional procedural approaches become difficult to manage due to scattered functions and global variables. OOP helps organize the code into self-contained objects that interact with each other in a structured way, making it easier to develop, debug, and extend.

Larger programs often require managing multiple components, each with its own **state and behavior**. For example, in an **automation system** controlling multiple devices like lights, fans, sensors, and actuators, OOP allows each device to be modeled as an individual class. This encapsulation ensures that each component can be modified independently without affecting other parts of the system.

Another key advantage of OOP is **inheritance**, which allows for the reuse of common code. Instead of rewriting code for every type of device, a base class can define general attributes and behaviors that all devices share. Child classes can then extend these functionalities, adding specialized behaviors where necessary. This makes the code more **modular** and **efficient**.

Consider a **factory automation system** where different types of machines, such as **conveyor belts, robotic arms, and temperature controllers**, need to be managed. Using OOP, a base Machine class can be created to define core attributes such as status (ON/OFF), power consumption, and start/stop behaviors.

Specific machine types can then inherit from this base class, adding unique functionalities like **speed control, temperature regulation, or movement mechanisms**.

Structuring a Larger Program with OOP

Let's design a **Python-based smart home system** using OOP principles. This system will manage multiple devices such as lights, fans, and temperature sensors, demonstrating how OOP simplifies program structure.

Step 1: Defining the Base Class for All Devices

The Device class serves as the foundation for all home devices, defining common behaviors like turning devices on or off.

```python
class Device:
    def __init__(self, name):
        self.name = name
        self.status = "OFF"

    def turn_on(self):
        self.status = "ON"
        print(f'{self.name} is now ON")

    def turn_off(self):
        self.status = "OFF"
        print(f'{self.name} is now OFF")
```

```python
    def get_status(self):
        return f"{self.name} is currently {self.status}"
```

Step 2: Creating Specific Device Classes

Each device type inherits from the Device class and adds its own specialized behavior.

```python
class Light(Device):
    def __init__(self, name, brightness=50):
        super().__init__(name)
        self.brightness = brightness

    def set_brightness(self, level):
        if 0 <= level <= 100:
            self.brightness = level
            print(f"{self.name} brightness set to {level}%")
        else:
            print("Invalid brightness level.")

class Fan(Device):
    def __init__(self, name, speed=1):
        super().__init__(name)
        self.speed = speed

    def set_speed(self, level):
        if 1 <= level <= 5:
            self.speed = level
            print(f"{self.name} speed set to level {level}")
        else:
            print("Invalid speed level.")

class TemperatureSensor(Device):
    def __init__(self, name, temperature=25):
```

```
        super().__init__(name)
        self.temperature = temperature

    def read_temperature(self):
        print(f"{self.name} reports temperature: {self.temperature}°C")
```

Step 3: Creating a Smart Home Controller

To manage multiple devices efficiently, we create a SmartHome class that acts as a **controller**.

```
class SmartHome:
    def __init__(self):
        self.devices = []

    def add_device(self, device):
        self.devices.append(device)

    def show_devices(self):
        for device in self.devices:
            print(device.get_status())
```

Step 4: Implementing the Smart Home System
```
# Creating devices
living_room_light = Light("Living Room Light")
bedroom_fan = Fan("Bedroom Fan")
temp_sensor   =   TemperatureSensor("Outdoor   Temperature
Sensor")

# Creating smart home system
my_home = SmartHome()

# Adding devices to the home
```

```
my_home.add_device(living_room_light)
my_home.add_device(bedroom_fan)
my_home.add_device(temp_sensor)

# Controlling devices
living_room_light.turn_on()
living_room_light.set_brightness(80)

bedroom_fan.turn_on()
bedroom_fan.set_speed(3)

temp_sensor.read_temperature()

# Displaying all device statuses
print("\nDevice Status Overview:")
my_home.show_devices()
```

Output of the Smart Home System

Living Room Light is now ON
Living Room Light brightness set to 80%
Bedroom Fan is now ON
Bedroom Fan speed set to level 3
Outdoor Temperature Sensor reports temperature: 25°C

Device Status Overview:
Living Room Light is currently ON
Bedroom Fan is currently ON
Outdoor Temperature Sensor is currently OFF

Hands-on Project: Designing a Python-Based Control System Simulation

Now, let's take this a step further by designing a **Python-based control system simulation** for an **industrial automation plant**. This system will simulate the operation of a **conveyor belt, robotic arm, and temperature controller**, demonstrating how OOP can be applied in real-world industrial systems.

Step 1: Creating a Base Class for Machines

```python
class Machine:
    def __init__(self, name):
        self.name = name
        self.status = "OFF"

    def start(self):
        self.status = "ON"
        print(f"{self.name} is now running.")

    def stop(self):
        self.status = "OFF"
        print(f"{self.name} has stopped.")

    def get_status(self):
        return f"{self.name} is currently {self.status}"
```

Step 2: Creating Specific Machines

```python
class ConveyorBelt(Machine):
    def __init__(self, name, speed=1):
        super().__init__(name)
        self.speed = speed
```

```python
    def set_speed(self, level):
        if 1 <= level <= 10:
            self.speed = level
            print(f"{self.name} speed set to level {level}")
        else:
            print("Invalid speed level.")

class RoboticArm(Machine):
    def __init__(self, name, position="Home"):
        super().__init__(name)
        self.position = position

    def move_to(self, position):
        self.position = position
        print(f"{self.name} moved to {position} position")

class TemperatureController(Machine):
    def __init__(self, name, temperature=25):
        super().__init__(name)
        self.temperature = temperature

    def set_temperature(self, temp):
        self.temperature = temp
        print(f"{self.name} set to {temp}°C")
```

Step 3: Simulating the Control System

```python
# Creating machines
belt = ConveyorBelt("Factory Conveyor Belt")
robot = RoboticArm("Assembly Robot")
temp_control = TemperatureController("Heat Chamber")

# Starting the machines
belt.start()
```

```
belt.set_speed(5)

robot.start()
robot.move_to("Pickup")

temp_control.start()
temp_control.set_temperature(75)

# Displaying status
print("\nMachine Status Overview:")
for machine in [belt, robot, temp_control]:
    print(machine.get_status())
```

Expected Output

```
Factory Conveyor Belt is now running.
Factory Conveyor Belt speed set to level 5
Assembly Robot is now running.
Assembly Robot moved to Pickup position
Heat Chamber is now running.
Heat Chamber set to 75°C

Machine Status Overview:
Factory Conveyor Belt is currently ON
Assembly Robot is currently ON
Heat Chamber is currently ON
```

Using OOP, we have structured a **large-scale control system simulation**, demonstrating how **classes, objects, and inheritance** help in organizing **real-world industrial processes**. This approach ensures that software systems remain **modular, scalable, and easy to maintain**, making them ideal for applications in **automation, robotics, smart homes, and IoT-based systems**.

Chapter 7

Python and Hardware – Interfacing with the Real World

Python has gained immense popularity in the field of **hardware interfacing and physical computing**, enabling enthusiasts, engineers, and researchers to interact with **microcontrollers, sensors, actuators, and embedded systems**. Unlike traditional embedded programming languages such as **C or Assembly**, Python simplifies hardware communication, making it accessible for beginners while remaining powerful enough for advanced users.

With Python, users can connect their computers to **microcontrollers like Arduino, Raspberry Pi, ESP8266, ESP32**, and other hardware platforms, allowing them to collect sensor data, control motors, blink LEDs, and automate real-world systems.

Hardware Interfacing Using Python

Interfacing Python with hardware is done through **communication protocols**, such as **Serial (UART), I2C, SPI, and GPIO (General Purpose Input/Output) pins**. Python provides several libraries that facilitate these interactions, allowing software to send and receive data from hardware components.

The following diagram provides an overview of how Python interfaces with hardware:

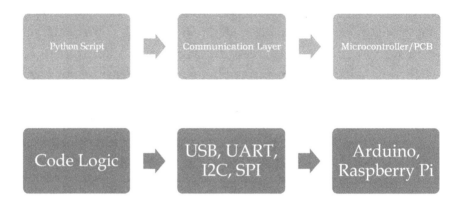

This structure enables a Python script to act as a **controller**, sending commands to a **microcontroller**, which then controls **LEDs, sensors, motors, and other devices**.

Common Python Libraries for Hardware Interfacing

Python provides several built-in and third-party libraries for **hardware communication**:

Library	Purpose	Supported Hardware
pyserial	Serial (UART) Communication	Arduino, ESP8266, ESP32, microcontrollers
RPi.GPIO	Control GPIO pins	Raspberry Pi

Library	Purpose	Supported Hardware
smbus	I2C Communication	Raspberry Pi, Arduino
spidev	SPI Communication	Raspberry Pi, Arduino
pyfirmata	Communicating with Arduino over Firmata protocol	Arduino

Among these, pyserial is one of the most widely used libraries, as it allows Python programs to communicate with external hardware via **Serial (UART) communication**.

Library pyserial for Serial Communication

Serial communication is the **most common method** of sending and receiving data between a computer and a microcontroller. **Arduino, ESP8266, ESP32, and many industrial controllers** use the UART (Universal Asynchronous Receiver-Transmitter) protocol to communicate with external devices.

What is Serial Communication?

Serial communication allows **data transmission one bit at a time** over a communication channel. It is used in many applications, such as **sending sensor**

readings from a microcontroller to a computer, controlling robots, and remote data logging.

How Serial Communication Works

When using Python for serial communication, the following parameters must be configured:

Parameter	Description	Common Values
Baud Rate	Speed of data transmission	9600, 115200
Data Bits	Number of bits per character	8
Stop Bits	Marks end of transmission	1
Parity Bit	Error-checking bit (optional)	None

Setting Up pyserial for Serial Communication

The pyserial library is used to communicate with devices via a serial port. It allows **Python scripts** to send and receive data from **Arduino, ESP32, and other microcontrollers**.

Step 1: Installing pyserial

Before using pyserial, install it using:

pip install pyserial

Step 2: Writing Python Code to Communicate with Arduino

The following Python script demonstrates **how to send and receive data** using pyserial.

```
import serial
import time

# Open the serial connection (Change COM port as per your system)
ser = serial.Serial('COM3', 9600, timeout=1)
time.sleep(2)  # Wait for the connection to establish

# Sending data to Arduino
ser.write(b'LED ON\n')  # Sending command
print("Sent: LED ON")

# Receiving data from Arduino
received_data = ser.readline().decode().strip()
print("Received:", received_data)

# Close the serial connection
ser.close()
```

This script performs the following actions:

1. **Opens a serial connection** to the microcontroller.
2. **Sends a command** ("LED ON") to the microcontroller.
3. **Receives a response** from the microcontroller.

4. **Closes the serial connection** after communication is complete.

Step 3: Writing the Arduino Code

The Arduino sketch below listens for commands from Python and **controls an LED accordingly**.

```
void setup() {
   Serial.begin(9600); // Start serial communication
   pinMode(13, OUTPUT); // Set pin 13 as output
}

void loop() {
   if (Serial.available() > 0) {
      String command = Serial.readStringUntil('\n'); // Read
incoming command

      if (command == "LED ON") {
         digitalWrite(13, HIGH); // Turn LED ON
         Serial.println("LED is ON");
      }
      else if (command == "LED OFF") {
         digitalWrite(13, LOW); // Turn LED OFF
         Serial.println("LED is OFF");
      }
   }
}
```

Step 4: Running the Python-Arduino Communication

1. **Upload the Arduino code** to an Arduino board (e.g., Arduino Uno).
2. **Connect the Arduino to the computer via USB.**
3. **Run the Python script.**
4. **Observe the LED on the Arduino turning ON and OFF based on Python commands.**

Expanding Serial Communication for IoT and Industrial Use

Using pyserial, Python can be used to **interface with industrial machines, IoT devices, and automation systems**. Here are some practical applications:

Application	Description
Home Automation	Controlling lights, fans, and appliances via Python scripts
Data Logging	Recording sensor data from temperature, humidity, and motion sensors
Industrial Automation	Communicating with PLCs (Programmable Logic Controllers) for factory automation
Remote Monitoring	Using IoT-based devices to monitor environmental conditions remotely

Interfacing Python with hardware using pyserial opens up endless possibilities for **home automation, robotics, industrial automation, and IoT projects**. By leveraging **serial communication**, users can develop Python applications that **control microcontrollers, collect real-time data, and automate physical systems**.

Basics of Raspberry Pi and Arduino Integration

Python is a powerful language that bridges the gap between software and hardware, enabling seamless integration with physical devices. Two of the most commonly used platforms for hardware projects are the **Raspberry Pi** and **Arduino**. While both are widely used in electronics and automation, they serve different purposes and have distinct architectures. Understanding their differences and how they complement each other is crucial for building real-world hardware applications using Python.

Understanding the Role of Raspberry Pi and Arduino

The **Arduino** is a microcontroller-based platform, meaning it is designed to execute simple tasks like reading sensor inputs, controlling LEDs, motors, and other components with precise timing. It does not run an operating system but instead executes compiled code written in C or Python-based libraries like pyFirmata.

On the other hand, the **Raspberry Pi** is a full-fledged microcomputer that runs a Linux-based operating system. It can perform complex tasks such as running servers, handling networking, and managing large-scale automation projects. Since it has built-in **USB, HDMI, Ethernet, and GPIO (General Purpose Input/Output) pins**, it is often used for projects requiring higher processing power, such as **computer vision, IoT applications, and AI-driven automation**.

The diagram below highlights their key differences:

Why Integrate Raspberry Pi with Arduino?

Since both platforms serve unique functions, integrating them allows users to leverage their **strengths**. The Raspberry Pi can handle high-level processing tasks, such as **data visualization, machine learning, or database management**, while the Arduino efficiently manages **real-time control tasks**, such as **reading sensor data and controlling motors or actuators**.

A common integration setup involves using the **Raspberry Pi as a central controller** that processes data and sends commands to **Arduino**, which directly interacts with the hardware components. The communication between them is typically established through **USB Serial (UART), I2C, or SPI protocols**.

Interfacing Arduino with Raspberry Pi

A **simple and widely used method** of communication between Raspberry Pi and Arduino is **Serial (UART) communication**, which allows the two devices to exchange data via USB or GPIO pins.

Step 1: Setting Up Serial Communication on Raspberry Pi

To establish communication, we must first enable the **serial interface** on the Raspberry Pi. This can be done using the **Raspberry Pi Configuration Tool**:

1. Open the terminal on the Raspberry Pi and enter:

   sudo raspi-config

2. Navigate to **Interfacing Options → Serial**.
3. Disable the login shell over serial but enable **serial hardware**.
4. Reboot the Raspberry Pi.

After enabling serial communication, install the required Python library:

pip install pyserial

Step 2: Writing Python Code on Raspberry Pi

Now, let's write a Python script on the Raspberry Pi to send data to the Arduino via **Serial communication**. The Raspberry Pi will send a command to the Arduino to turn a **motor ON or OFF**.

```
import serial
import time
```

```
# Open serial connection (Change '/dev/ttyUSB0' based on your
setup)
ser = serial.Serial('/dev/ttyUSB0', 9600, timeout=1)
time.sleep(2)  # Allow time for connection to establish

# Sending command to Arduino
command = "MOTOR ON\n"
ser.write(command.encode())  # Convert string to bytes and send
print("Sent:", command)

# Receiving acknowledgment from Arduino
response = ser.readline().decode().strip()
print("Arduino Response:", response)

# Closing the serial connection
ser.close()
```

Step 3: Writing the Arduino Code

On the Arduino side, we will write a program that
listens for commands from the Raspberry Pi via serial
communication and controls a **DC motor using a
relay module**.

```
int motorPin = 9;  // Connect relay module or transistor switch to
this pin

void setup() {
    Serial.begin(9600); // Start serial communication
    pinMode(motorPin, OUTPUT); // Set motor pin as output
}

void loop() {
```

```
  if (Serial.available() > 0) {
    String command = Serial.readStringUntil('\n');  // Read
incoming command

    if (command == "MOTOR ON") {
      digitalWrite(motorPin, HIGH); // Turn Motor ON
      Serial.println("Motor is ON");
    }
    else if (command == "MOTOR OFF") {
      digitalWrite(motorPin, LOW); // Turn Motor OFF
      Serial.println("Motor is OFF");
    }
  }
}
```

Hands-on Project: Controlling a Motor Using Python and a Microcontroller

This project demonstrates how **Python running on a Raspberry Pi can control a DC motor connected to an Arduino**. The Raspberry Pi acts as a **controller**, while the Arduino executes real-time commands. This is a fundamental concept used in **robotics, home automation, and industrial automation**.

Hardware Components Required

Component	Specification
Raspberry Pi	Any model (RPi 3, 4, or Zero W)

Component	Specification
Arduino	Uno, Nano, or Mega
DC Motor	12V or 6V motor
Relay Module	5V Single Channel Relay
Power Supply	12V DC for Motor, 5V for Arduino
Jumper Wires	Male-to-Male and Male-to-Female wires

Circuit Connection

The following circuit connections are made between the **Arduino, motor, and relay module**:

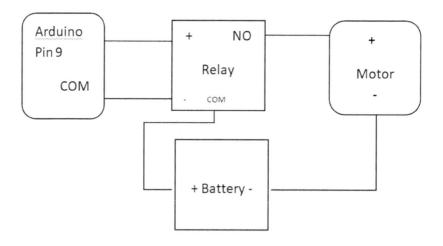

1. **Arduino Digital Pin 9 → Relay Module Input**

2. **Relay Module NO (Normally Open) Terminal** → **Motor Positive Terminal**
3. **Relay Module COM (Common) Terminal** → **12V Power Source Positive**
4. **Motor Negative Terminal** → **12V Power Source Negative**
5. **Relay Module Ground** → **Arduino Ground**

Working of the Project

1. **Python script on Raspberry Pi** sends commands via serial communication.
2. **Arduino receives the command** and activates the **relay module** to turn the motor ON or OFF.
3. The **motor starts running or stops based on the command** received from Python.

Testing the System

1. Upload the **Arduino sketch** to the Arduino board.
2. Run the **Python script** on the Raspberry Pi.
3. Observe the **motor turning ON and OFF** based on the commands sent from Python.

Real-World Applications of This Project

Integrating Python with microcontrollers like **Arduino and Raspberry Pi** opens the door to **industrial automation, robotics, IoT applications, and smart home systems**. Some **real-world use cases** include:

Application	Description
Automated Fan Control	Control a fan based on temperature readings from a sensor
Smart Irrigation System	Activate water pumps for irrigation using sensor data
Industrial Motor Control	Remotely turn motors ON/OFF for automation
Robot Navigation	Use motors for robot movement controlled by Python scripts

By integrating **Raspberry Pi and Arduino**, Python can be used to build **smart, interactive systems** that bridge the gap between **software and physical hardware**. This chapter provided an in-depth understanding of **serial communication**, **hardware integration**, and **motor control using Python**.

Advanced Topics and Final Project

Python is not just a programming language for simple scripts; it is a vast ecosystem that connects software with real-world applications. By understanding how to work with **APIs, web requests, and graphical user interfaces (GUIs)**, one can build dynamic, interactive applications that can control hardware, automate tasks, and even create full-fledged software solutions.

This chapter will focus on **working with APIs, sending web requests, and designing graphical interfaces using Tkinter**, which will be essential for creating real-world projects.

Working with APIs and Web Requests

An **API (Application Programming Interface)** allows different software applications to communicate with each other. APIs are widely used in modern applications, from fetching weather updates and financial data to controlling IoT devices remotely. In Python, the requests library is a powerful tool for making HTTP requests to interact with APIs.

Understanding HTTP Requests

When two systems communicate over the web, they use HTTP requests. The four most common types of requests are:

HTTP Method	Description
GET	Retrieves data from an API (e.g., fetching weather details)

HTTP Method	Description
POST	Sends new data to an API (e.g., uploading files or submitting forms)
PUT	Updates existing data on a server
DELETE	Removes data from a server

For instance, if we want to retrieve current weather information, we can use a free weather API such as **OpenWeatherMap** and send a GET request.

Fetching Data from an API using Python

To begin, the requests library needs to be installed:

pip install requests

A simple example of fetching weather data using OpenWeatherMap API is:

import requests

```
API_KEY = "your_api_key"  # Replace with a real API key
CITY = "New York"
URL                                                      =
f"https://api.openweathermap.org/data/2.5/weather?q={CITY}&a
ppid={API_KEY}"
```

```python
response = requests.get(URL)  # Sending GET request
data = response.json()  # Parsing the JSON response

if response.status_code == 200:
    temperature = data['main']['temp'] - 273.15  # Convert from Kelvin to Celsius
    weather = data['weather'][0]['description']
    print(f"Current weather in {CITY}: {weather}, Temperature: {temperature:.2f}°C")
else:
    print("Failed to retrieve data")
```

Using APIs for IoT and Hardware Projects

APIs are essential in IoT applications where devices communicate over the internet. For example, a **Python script can send sensor data to a cloud server** or fetch information from a database to make real-time decisions. Some real-world applications include:

1. **Home Automation:** Using a cloud-based API to control lights and appliances remotely.
2. **Weather Monitoring Stations:** Sending temperature and humidity readings to an API for analysis.
3. **Industrial Automation:** Fetching machine status and production data via web requests.

To demonstrate, imagine an IoT project where a **Raspberry Pi fetches sensor data and updates an online dashboard**. The API request might look like this:

```
import requests
sensor_data = {"temperature": 25, "humidity": 60}
URL = "https://example.com/update-sensor"

response = requests.post(URL, json=sensor_data)  # Sending data
to API
print("Server Response:", response.text)
```

By mastering APIs, one can integrate Python with real-world data sources, enabling automation, remote monitoring, and even AI-based decision-making.

Introduction to GUI Programming with Tkinter

While command-line applications are powerful, **Graphical User Interfaces (GUIs)** make software more user-friendly. Python's **Tkinter** library provides a simple yet effective way to create desktop applications with interactive buttons, text fields, and other UI elements.

Why Use Tkinter?

1. **Built-in with Python** – No need for additional installation.
2. **Lightweight** – Runs smoothly even on low-power devices like Raspberry Pi.
3. **Easy to Use** – Provides a simple way to build graphical applications.

Creating a Basic Tkinter Window

A **basic GUI application** starts by importing the tkinter module and creating a main window.

```
import tkinter as tk

# Creating the main window
root = tk.Tk()
root.title("Simple GUI")
root.geometry("300x200")

# Running the application
root.mainloop()
```

Adding Widgets to the GUI

A GUI is made up of **widgets**, which are interactive elements like buttons, labels, and text boxes. The example below demonstrates how to create a **simple temperature converter** from Celsius to Fahrenheit using Tkinter.

```
import tkinter as tk

def convert():
    celsius = float(entry.get())
    fahrenheit = (celsius * 9/5) + 32
    result_label.config(text=f'{fahrenheit:.2f} °F")

# Creating GUI window
root = tk.Tk()
root.title("Temperature Converter")

# Adding Widgets
```

```
entry_label = tk.Label(root, text="Enter Temperature (°C):")
entry_label.pack()

entry = tk.Entry(root)
entry.pack()

convert_button          =          tk.Button(root,          text="Convert",
command=convert)
convert_button.pack()

result_label = tk.Label(root, text="")
result_label.pack()

# Running the application
root.mainloop()
```

This script creates a simple **temperature converter** where the user enters a value in Celsius, and clicking the **Convert** button displays the temperature in Fahrenheit.

Hands-on Final Project: Smart Home Control Panel

Project Overview

To bring together the topics covered in this chapter, we will build a **Smart Home Control Panel** using **Tkinter for GUI, APIs for data retrieval, and Raspberry Pi for hardware control**.

The control panel will:

1. **Display real-time weather data** using OpenWeatherMap API.
2. **Control an LED or a relay switch** using Raspberry Pi GPIO.

Step 1: Setting Up Tkinter GUI

First, create the main window and layout for the smart home control panel.

```python
import tkinter as tk
import requests
import RPi.GPIO as GPIO

# GPIO setup
LED_PIN = 18
GPIO.setmode(GPIO.BCM)
GPIO.setup(LED_PIN, GPIO.OUT)

def toggle_led():
    if GPIO.input(LED_PIN):
        GPIO.output(LED_PIN, GPIO.LOW)
        led_button.config(text="Turn LED ON")
    else:
        GPIO.output(LED_PIN, GPIO.HIGH)
        led_button.config(text="Turn LED OFF")

def get_weather():
    API_KEY = "your_api_key"
    CITY = "New York"
    URL = f'https://api.openweathermap.org/data/2.5/weather?q={CITY}&appid={API_KEY}"
```

```python
    response = requests.get(URL)
    data = response.json()

    if response.status_code == 200:
        temp = data['main']['temp'] - 273.15
        weather_label.config(text=f"Weather:
{data['weather'][0]['description']}, {temp:.2f} °C")
    else:
        weather_label.config(text="Failed to fetch weather")

# Creating GUI
root = tk.Tk()
root.title("Smart Home Control Panel")

weather_button    =    tk.Button(root,    text="Get    Weather",
command=get_weather)
weather_button.pack()

weather_label = tk.Label(root, text="")
weather_label.pack()

led_button    =    tk.Button(root,    text="Turn    LED    ON",
command=toggle_led)
led_button.pack()

root.mainloop()
```

This chapter covered **APIs, web requests, and GUI programming**, essential skills for building dynamic, real-world applications. The **final project demonstrated how Python can be used to create a Smart Home Control Panel** that retrieves live weather data and controls physical hardware.

THE END

www.ingramcontent.com/pod-product-compliance
Lightning Source LLC
LaVergne TN
LVHW051657050326
832903LV00032B/3871